Weaving Country Baskets

Maryanne Gillooly

CONTENTS

A Word to New Basket Makers

The ancient art of basket making continues to delight crafters today. Its combination of function and beauty make this craft particularly rewarding. The flower-gathering basket and herb basket are unique projects for those interested in creating new and original baskets.

Although these projects are recommended for those with some basket-making experience, with careful reading and attention to the diagrams a beginner may also be successful. Basketry is an acquired skill, but its methods are simple and straightforward. There are no real rules or limitations, so do not hesitate to alter these designs, materials, and methods. Develop your own personal style to make your baskets unique works of art.

A list of sources, tools, and basket-making kits can be found on page 31.

There are two basic processes you will need to understand before you begin weaving. The first is *four-fold lashing,* the weaving that binds hoops together to form the most basic framework of a basket. The second is *dyeing,* the process of coloring reed. Mastering these two techniques will allow you to weave sturdy and colorful country baskets.

Four-Fold Lashing

Four-fold lashing is a relatively simple form of weaving baskets that creates a classic diamond pattern in the structure of the basket. The step-by-step instructions and diagrams below outline the basic pattern of this weaving technique. You will use this technique for both the flower-gathering basket and the herb basket.

Step A. Reed has both a right side and a wrong side. The right side is smooth and the wrong side is rough. If one end of the reed is bent back and forth, the wrong side can quickly be identified as it will split and fray.

Begin by having one of the crossed sections of the hoops facing you. Be sure the handle is in the upright position. Then, with the wrong side of the reed facing out, place the piece of pliable reed behind the oval handle hoops. Leave about an inch at the end so that it may be tucked into the weaving as the lashing progresses. Fold at point 2 so that the right side of the reed now faces up. Bring the reed across and up to the rim on the right hand side of the handle to point 3, then straight down and behind the rim to point 4.

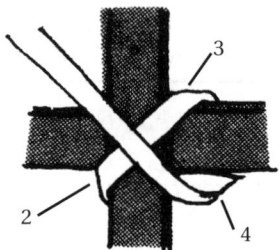

Step B. From point 4, bring the reed up and across to point 5, then behind the two oval handle hoops to point 6. You have now formed an X across the hoops. Keeping the reed next to the previous row, bring the reed down and across to point 7.

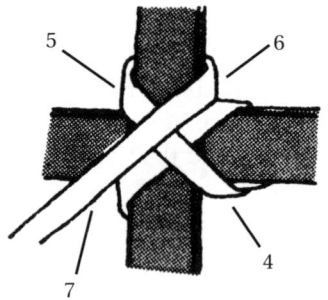

Step C. From point 7, bring the reed straight up and behind the rim to point 8. Then, bring it down and across to point 9, and behind the handle bottom to point 10.

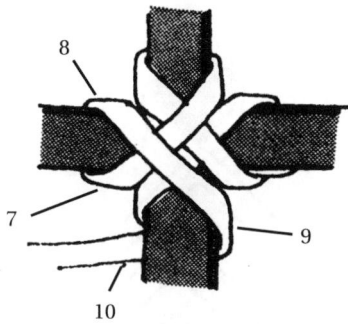

Step D. The reed must then be brought up and across to point 11, then straight down and behind the rim to point 12. Bring the reed up and across to point 13.

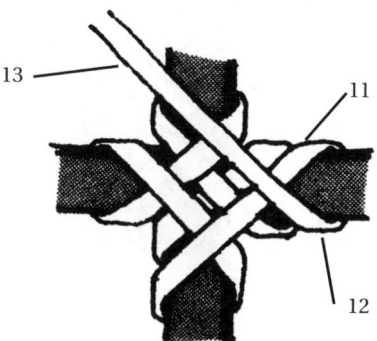

At this point you can see the diamond shape of the four-fold lashing. Continue this process of wrapping, making sure that each row overlaps the other slightly and that the reed always lies flat against the hoops. It helps to push down hard with your fingertips at every crossover.

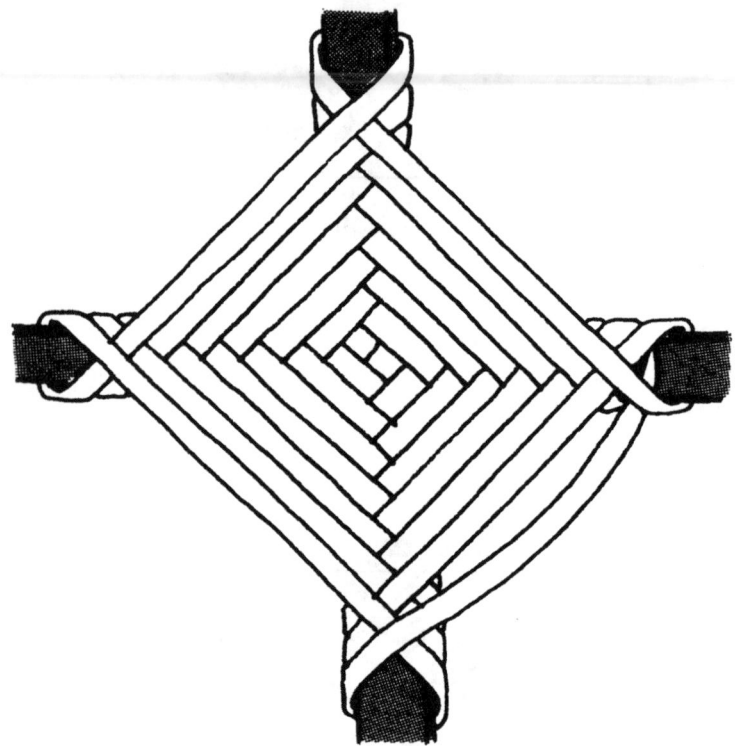

Completed four-fold lashing.

Finish the lashing by cutting the end of the reed at an angle with scissors and inserting it under the last row at one of the corners. Wrap the reed behind the oval hoops, leaving about 1 inch at the end of the reed. Then bend the reed so that the wrong side is facing out and firmly tuck the end into the base of the lashing. Then repeat the lashing on the other side of the basket.

How to Dye Reed

The easiest and the fastest way to dye reed is with packaged commercial fabric dye. One small package of dye (1⅛ ounces) will dye about 1 pound of reed. Mix the dye according to package instructions, using hot water right from the tap. You can mix the dye in a stainless-steel kitchen sink, old pot, or any other metal container. Stir until well dissolved. You must wet the reed before placing it in the dye bath. Leave the material in until it is the shade you want (don't forget that it will look lighter when it dries).

If you like, leave some reed in the dye for about 30 minutes, replace it with some that you leave in for about 15 minutes, and then replace that with some that you dye for just a few minutes. That will give you three shades of the same color.

Remove the reed from the dye bath with a stick or an old wooden spoon, rinse it in clear water, and place it on lots of paper towels to drain. Then hang it to dry completely. You may hang it inside or outside, as long as it is out of the sun.

When dyed reed is soaked later for weaving, some color may come out. Use separate soaking buckets for each color.

If you have a large pot, you can dye a finished basket. First, try a test piece of reed to make certain the color is right. Then wet the basket, place it in the dye bath, and stir it gently with a stick. Take the basket out when it reaches the right shade, pat it with paper towels, and hang it up to dry. Leave some towels underneath to catch the drippings.

Natural Dyes. Using dyes from natural materials requires time and patience, but is rewarding. The only dyeing material that I know of that does not call for a mordant (fixative) to keep a permanent true color is black walnut hulls. The colors obtained from other natural materials, without using a mordant, are not as long-lasting or vivid as the colors of commercially packaged dyes, but paler and more subtle. I prefer them that way and feel better not using the many chemicals required in mordanting.

To use black walnut hulls as a dye, soak ½ pound of the hulls overnight in 3 to 4 gallons of water. The next day, boil the hulls in the water for an hour. Let the mixture cool, and then strain through cheesecloth to separate the dye from the hulls.

To get a darker brown dye, try using more hulls or less water. This procedure can also be used with coffee, tea, or any other natural materials you may wish to experiment with.

Definition of Terms

Breaking down, weaving over a series of tightly spaced ribs as if they were one rib until there is enough space between them to weave through.

D-hoop, hoop with one flat edge.

Filling in, weaving incomplete rows to fill the basket framework so that the weaving from one side of the basket to the other can progress in a straight line. Also called "stepping."

Handle, the top portion of the vertical hoop.

Handle bottom, the bottom portion of the vertical hoop.

Lashing, the weaving used to bind two hoops together.

Ribs, also known as "spokes." These are the round reeds that form the framework of the basket and provide the warp to weave over and under.

Rim, the horizontal hoop that forms the edge of the basket.

Weaver, the piece of reed or other material used to weave.

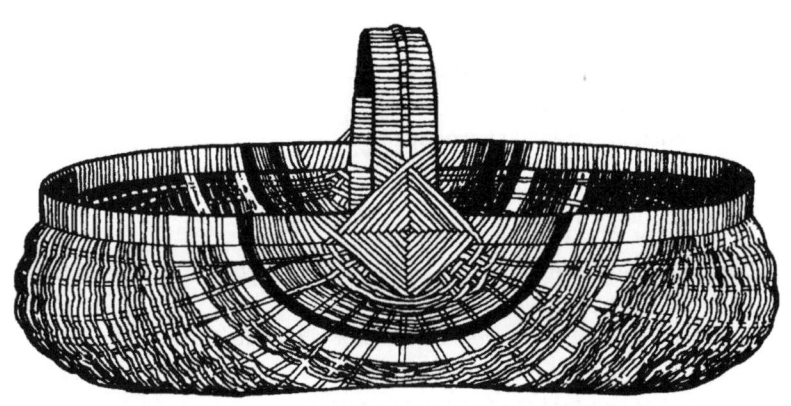

Flower-Gathering Basket

The shape and pattern of the flower-gathering basket make for an attractive variation to basic basket making. This particular design calls for using both flat and round reeds in shades of blue, lavender, and natural. However, any colors you wish to use may be substituted. If you prefer, the basket may also be woven in any single color.

The basic construction involves forming the handles and rim of the basket from oval and D-hoops, respectively. The flat sides of the D-hoops create a wooden piece across the center that helps to hold flower stems down into the basket. The flowers themselves drape out on either side of the basket.

The flower-gathering basket is a beautiful, functional basket that you should enjoy making as much as you will using and displaying it.

Tools & Materials for Flower-Gathering Basket

Tools:

> **Garden clippers or scissors**
> **Twist ties or string**
> **Pencil and pencil sharpener**
> **Tape measure**
> **Bucket**

Optional: *Spray Acrylic* (basket may be sprayed with a coat or two when it is completed)
Linseed Oil (*before* the basket is woven, the handles and rim may be treated with the oil to darken the color of the oak and bring out the grain)

Materials:
Hoops:
2 oak oval-shaped hoops, 8" by 12" size, for framework
2 oak D-hoops, 8" by 12" size, for framework

Ribs:
1 bundle #7 round reed

Dye (unless you choose not to use color):
1 package of each color — light blue, dark blue, royal blue, and lavender

Weavers:
2 bundles ³⁄₁₆" flat reed
1 bundle #2 round reed

Dye the weavers as follows (or leave undyed for an all-natural look):

> Royal Blue: 1 bundle ³⁄₁₆" flat reed
> Light Blue: 2 strands ³⁄₁₆" flat reed and 6 strands #2 round reed
> Dark Blue: 6 strands #2 round reed
> Lavender: 6 strands #2 round reed
> Natural: 12 strands ³⁄₁₆" flat reed

Step 1. Framework

To begin, secure the two D-hoops together. They should be placed flat end to flat end and tied together with a twist tie or some string.

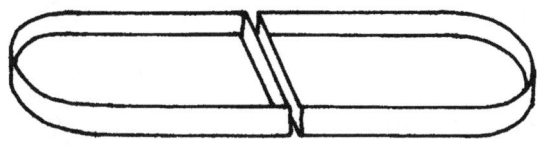

The two oval hoops should be placed inside and perpendicular to the two D-hoops, against the flat areas. Make sure that the oval hoops are even with each other. They should be placed within the D-hoops so that slightly more than half of the oval hoops (about 16 inches) is below the D-hoops and slightly less (about 13 inches) is above. This should be measured and marked with a pencil.

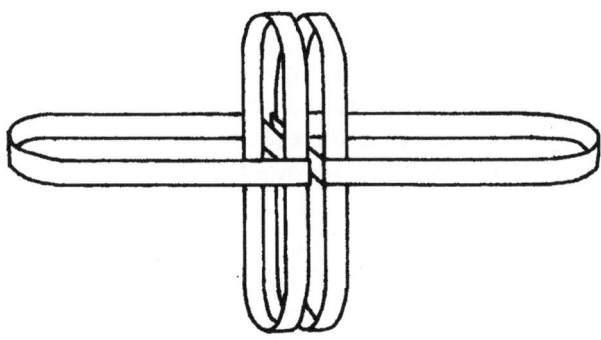

Step 2. Four-Fold Lashing

The four hoops are now ready to be secured with a four-fold lashing. First, soak a strand of $\frac{1}{16}$-inch flat natural reed until it is pliable. This should be done in a bucket of warm water and will take about four to five minutes. Do not soak the reed too long or it will fray and crack.

Follow the instructions for four-fold lashing that begin on page 3. Complete ten full rows of lashing, ending at the base where you began. Rows can be counted on the back, behind the lashing.

Because the hoops are so wide and the basket has a double handle, you may find it necessary to add in a new piece of reed to complete the lashing. If so, tuck the end of the old reed through the previous row, near a corner where there is a crossover. Next, take a new piece of soaked, pliable reed and slide the end through the last row, right on top of the old piece. Make sure the *wrong* side is facing out. Bend the new piece of reed over so that the right side is facing you and continue the lashing.

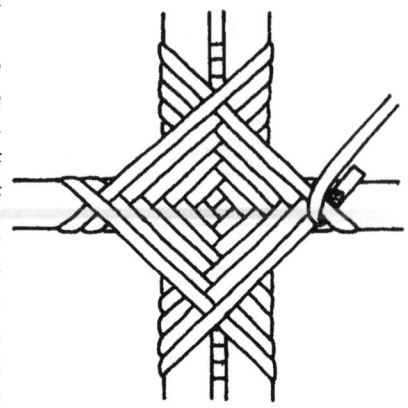

Tuck the old and new ends of the reed under the last row.

Step 3. Structure

You will now need to form the structure of the basket by placing in the ribs. They will create a sturdy framework for your weaving. Start by cutting a set of three ribs for each side of the basket, for a total of six ribs. Cut the #7 round reed into these approximate lengths:

> First rib — 30 inches long
> Second rib — 30 inches long
> Third rib — 16 inches long

Each rib should be cut at an angle or sharpened with a pencil sharpener so it will fit snugly behind the lashing. Be sure to *lay* each rib behind the lashing. If you push them in, they will pierce the front of the lashing.

With this in mind, begin with the first set of three ribs. Place the first rib just below the rim, with each end resting behind the lashing on either side of the basket. The second rib is placed in the center. The third rib is placed at the base near the bottom of the oval hoops (see illustration on page 13). Repeat the rib placement on the other side of the basket.

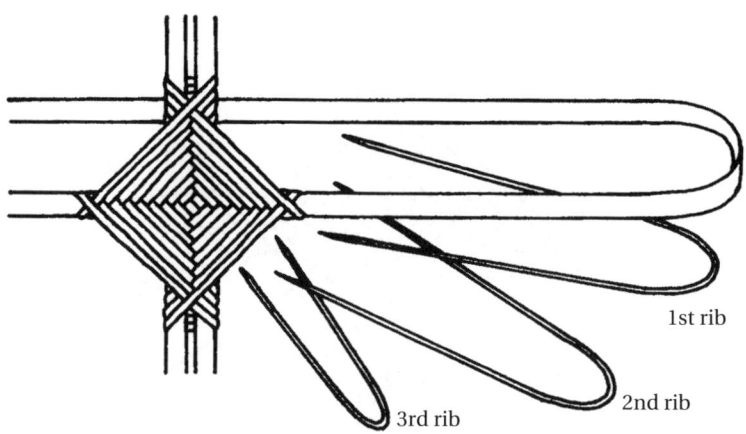

1st rib

2nd rib

3rd rib

Place the first rib just below the rim, with each end resting behind the lashing on either side of the basket. Place the second rib in the center, and the third at the base near the bottom of the oval hoops.

Step 4. Weaving

The basic framework of the basket is now in place. The hoops are firmly joined by the four-fold lashing and the ribs are evenly spaced and firmly in place. The weaving is done in a simple over-one, under-one pattern. However, in the beginning, there will not be enough space between the ribs to weave in and out. Therefore, a process called *breaking down* must first be followed.

Begin the weaving with a new piece of ³⁄₁₆-inch flat natural reed that has been soaked for a few minutes in warm water. Tuck the end, *wrong* side facing out, into the space at the base of the lashing. Bend it over so that the right side is facing you and begin weaving to the right. Weave under all three ribs, treating them as a single unit. Wrap the reed over and around the rim, then back down and over all three ribs. Weave under the two bottom sections of the oval hoops. Be sure to bring the reed tightly up and behind the lashing so that it fits snugly, without any gaps. Weave over all three ribs on the left side, then weave under and around the rim. Weave back down and under all three ribs, then weave over the hoops to the base of the lashing where you began. You have now completed one full row of weaving (see illustration on page 14).

The first row of weaving.

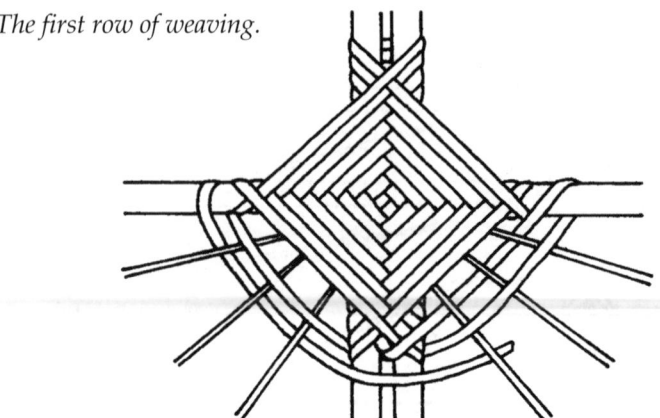

Continue weaving the next row with the same piece of reed by going under the first rib, over the second, and under the third. Weave over and around the rim, back down and over one rib, under the next, and over the last. Weave under both hoops to the other side, weave over one rib, under the next, and over the last. Weave under and around the rim, back down and under one rib, over the next, under the last, and over the two handle hoops to the beginning again.

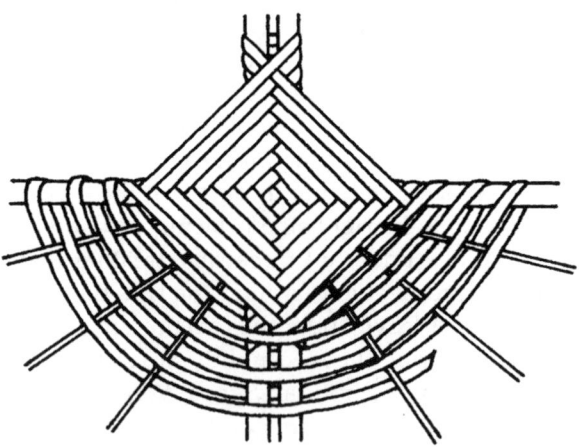

Three full rows of weaving.

Complete three full rows of weaving with the flat natural reed. Cut the reed (unless you have chosen not to add color — in that case, leave the reed uncut), leaving a 1- to 2-inch extension to the right (see illustration on page 14). Repeat the first three rows of weaving on the other side of the basket.

round reed

round reed

At this point, two pieces of round reed need to be added between the two oval hoops, at the handle and the bottom sections of the basket. The first should be cut to 14 inches in length and placed between the top handle sections of the hoops. The second should be cut to 16 inches in length and placed between the bottom sections of the hoops. This will help to fill the space between the two hoops and should be woven through from now on.

New ribs must now be added to create more framework for the basket. The new ribs should fit directly under each existing rib. They should be cut and tapered so that they slide into the weaving and rest evenly against the upper rib. They should be just long enough to fit snugly, but need not be pushed in as far as the lashing.

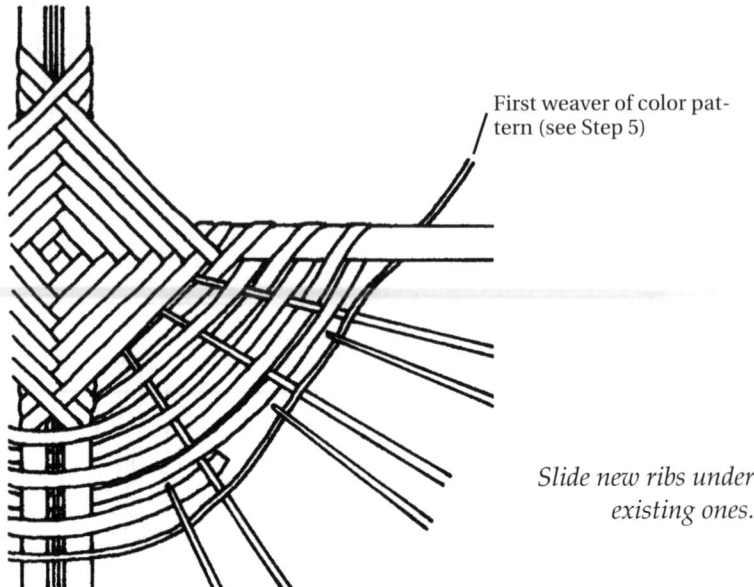

First weaver of color pattern (see Step 5)

Slide new ribs under existing ones.

From #7 round reed, cut two sets of three ribs each. The lengths may vary but you should cut each piece approximately:

First rib — 26 inches long

Second rib — 21 inches long

Third rib — 14 inches long

Taper each end and slide the new ribs into the weaving right next to and under each existing rib.

Slide the remaining set of additional ribs into the other side of the basket. There should now be six ribs on each side for a total of twelve ribs in the basket.

Step 5. Color

Now the color pattern can be introduced into the basket. If you have chosen not to add color to your basket, you did not cut the piece of reed you ended with. Continue to weave, following the rest of the basic instructions, with the same piece of flat natural reed, weaving over the new ribs until you run out of reed. Then add in a new weaver (see box on page 17) and continue.

Introducing New Reed

There are two ways to introduce new reed into your weaving. If you are going to introduce round reed into your weaving, you should lay the round reed next to the end of the reed you have just finished with (see illustration on page 16). This also holds true if you are going to match a length of flat reed to the end of a round reed. However, if you are going to introduce a flat reed into your weaving, and the reed you have just finished with is also a flat reed, you should lay the new reed on top of the old reed.

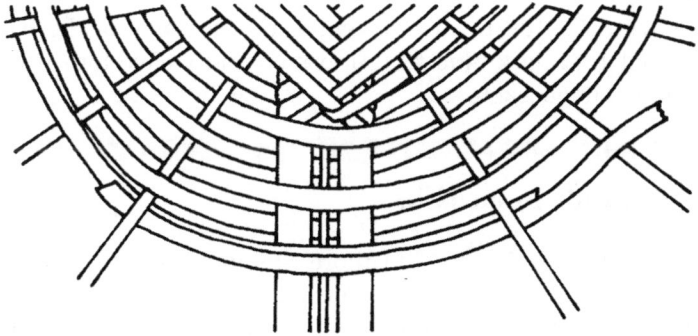

To introduce a new or colored flat reed into existing flat reed weaving, lay the new reed on top of the old reed.

If you are adding the color pattern, start with a soaked strand of light blue #2 round reed. Place the end of the reed right next to the flat natural reed.

Weave over the hoops, under the new rib to the right, over the next rib, under the new one, over the old one, under the new one, over the old one, under the rim, and around and back under the rib. Weave over the next rib, under one, over one, under one, over one, and under one hoop. Then weave over the new piece of round reed and under the other hoop to the other side. Continue weaving over the next rib, under one, over one, under one, over one, under one, then over the rim. Then weave around back down and over one, under one, over one, under one, and under one. Weave over the hoop, under the piece of round reed between the hoops, and over the next hoop. Continue in this pattern with the light blue round reed for five rows. Leave a few inches of overlap before you cut it. Repeat this pattern of five rows of light blue on the other side of the basket.

Switch to lavender #2 round reed. Lay the new piece of round reed right next to the old one. Tuck the end of the new reed under the rib to the left of the handle bottom. Let the two reeds lie double until you start weaving with the new piece toward the right side of the basket.

Weave three full rows of lavender on each side of the basket. Then, switch to dark blue #2 round reed and weave four rows on each side of the basket.

Step 6. Additional Ribs

You will now need to add more ribs to the framework of the basket. Add one rib between each existing rib. Cut two sets of five ribs each from #7 round reed. Each rib should be tapered so that it will slide snugly into the weave underneath. Cut each piece as follows:

> First rib — 24 inches long
> Second rib — 22 inches long
> Third rib — 20 inches long
> Fourth rib — 15 inches long
> Fifth rib — 12 inches long

Add the five new ribs as shown on page 19. Repeat the placement on the other side. There should now be eleven ribs on each side for a total of twenty-two ribs in the basket.

When you add these ribs, it is important that you check the shape and curve of the basket. You may need to push or pull some ribs in and out slightly. Any ribs that are too short may need to be replaced with longer ones. Long ribs may need to be cut again. The length of the new ribs should be in between the length of the two ribs next to it. Continue to eye the shape so that an even, rounded curve is maintained.

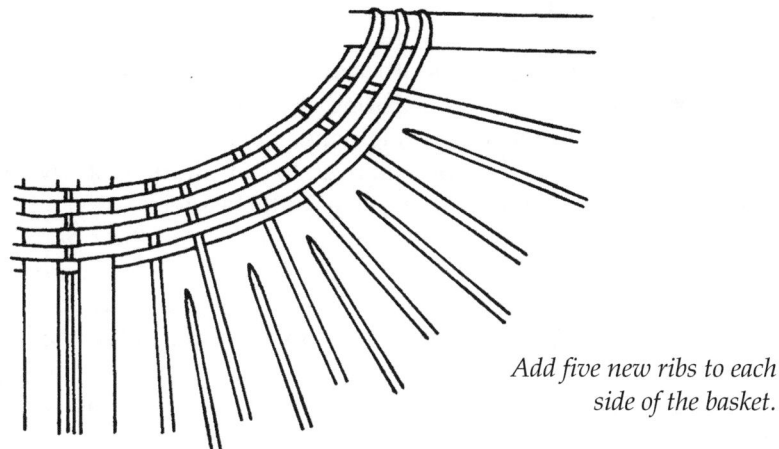

*Add five new ribs to each
side of the basket.*

Now change to a piece of soaked natural ³⁄₁₆-inch flat reed. Weave one complete row on each side. Be sure to include the new ribs in the weaving. Then weave one row of light blue ³⁄₁₆-inch flat reed on each side of the basket. Weave three rows of the royal blue ³⁄₁₆-inch flat reed on each side, followed by one row of natural ³⁄₁₆-inch flat reed on each side. This completes the color pattern. The rest of the basket is woven in the royal blue flat ³⁄₁₆-inch reed.

Color Pattern Chart

3 rows — natural flat reed
5 rows — light blue round reed
3 rows — lavender round reed
4 rows — dark blue round reed
1 row — natural flat reed
1 row — light blue flat reed
3 rows — royal blue flat reed
1 row — natural flat reed

Continue weaving the rest of the basket in the royal blue flat reed. Add in new royal blue weavers as needed.

Step 7. Filling In

After weaving three rows of royal blue, you will find that the bottom section of the basket is getting closer to being finished. It is necessary to get the weaving straightened out so that the center can be woven straight across. You will need to start filling in the weaving by trying to "catch up" on the sides of the basket.

In order to achieve this, you must weave up to the rim, back down to the ninth rib near the bottom, and wrap the weaver around that rib. Then weave back up to the rim again. Do not weave over to the other side. Weave around the rim and start back down again to the eighth row. Wrap the reed around that rib and weave back up to the rim again. This gradual shortening of your weaving row is called *stepping.*

Continuing in this fashion, gradually fill in the section on the right side of the basket. Once you have filled in four or five rows, weave down and across the handle bottom to the left side of the basket. Fill in the left side as you did the right side. Weave back down to the bottom of the handle and stop there. Repeat this on the other side of the basket to keep the shape of the basket even and balanced.

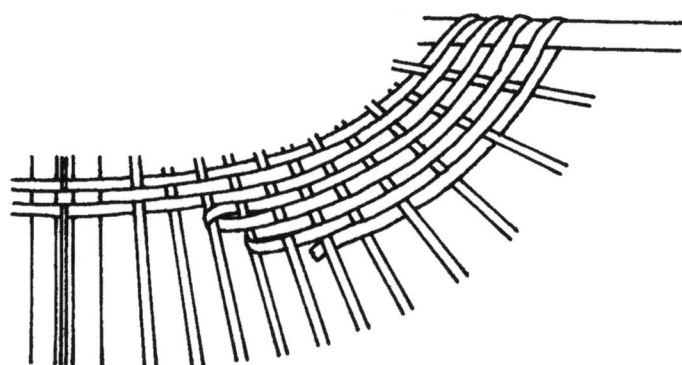

Filling in is necessary to straighten out the weaving before adding the colored reed.

Step 8. Additional Ribs

You will now need to add ribs one last time. Cut two sets of four ribs in the following lengths from #7 round reed, and place as follows:

First rib — 17 inches long, placed under first rib
Second rib — 17 inches long, placed under third rib
Third rib — 15 inches long, placed under fifth rib
Fourth rib — 12 inches long, placed under seventh rib

Again, cut each rib at an angle so that it can slide into the weaving. Each side should now have fifteen ribs for a grand total of thirty ribs in the basket.

Add a row or two of even weaving with the royal blue flat reed, including the new ribs in the weaving. Soon you will notice that the weaving at the rim is nearing completion. At this point you will need to fill in again. This filling in is done close to the rim, but does not include weaving over the rim.

Weave down to the seventh rib. Wrap the weaver around it and weave back up to the third rib. Do not weave up to the rim. Weave back down to the sixth rib, wrap the reed around it, and weave back up to the fourth rib. Then weave all the way down to the other side of the basket and repeat the filling in on the left side. Repeat this process for the other side of the basket.

Filling in is the most difficult part of making this style of basket. This is where experience is helpful, because there are no hard and fast rules or specific guidelines to follow. However, if you continue to look at the shape of the basket and the lines of the weaving, you will start to grasp this process. The idea is to make the *unfilled* space look like a straight, even area to complete the weaving in. Do not hesitate to try a new way or to add another row of filling in.

Finish by weaving in the middle area. Continue to weave from one side to the other until the two sides meet in the middle. Ideally, you should be able to overlap the ends from each side, just like when you add a new weaver. Be sure the pattern remains in an alternating over-and-under weave as the weavers meet in the center of the basket. You may need to push the weaving apart to make space for one last row, if necessary.

Step 9. Handle

Start the handle with a piece of soaked royal blue ³⁄₁₆-inch flat reed. Beginning at the top of the lashing, place the reed end into the space at the top with the wrong side up. Fold it over so the right side is showing and bend it to the left of the handle. Wrap around and behind the first hoop, bringing the reed through and over the center piece of round reed. Weave under and back over the second hoop, under the round reed, and over the other hoop. Again, wrap the reed around the outside edge of the handle and weave under the hoop, over the round reed, and under the other hoop.

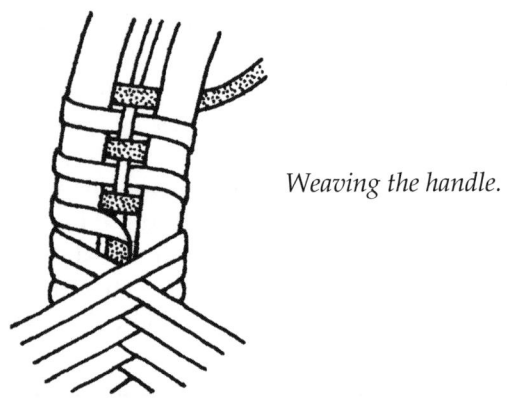

Weaving the handle.

Continue in this manner, weaving all the way around the handle to the lashing on the other side. Finish the edge by cutting the reed just long enough to turn wrong-side up, and tuck the end into the top of the lashing.

Step 10. Finishing

Be sure to trim and clip any stray ends of reed. A coat of acrylic spray paint will help to hold the color longer and protect the basket. Feel free to experiment with any of these materials and directions, as they are simply meant to be general guidelines. You will need to make adjustments according to your own needs and unique basket-weaving style.

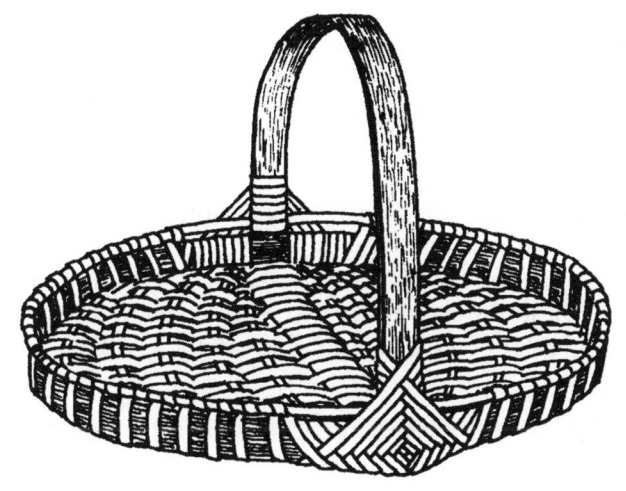

Herb Basket

This basket is called an herb basket because of its shape. Generally, herbs are dried on low, flat baskets. It is a functional, sturdy basket that can be woven in a fairly short time. The wide D-hoop makes the handle very strong, and the wider rim allows for the basket to be deep enough to serve as a marvelous handled tray.

The directions include a color pattern similar to that for the flower-gathering basket. Like the flower-gathering basket, it is also appealing when woven entirely of natural reed.

Step 1. Framework

The oval hoop forms the rim of the basket and the D-hoop creates the handle of the basket. Place the oval hoop inside the D-hoop and slide it approximately halfway through, so that it looks evenly spaced on each side of the handle. If you measure with a measuring tape, each side should be about 16½ inches around (see illustration on page 25).

Tools & Materials
for Herb Basket

Tools:

>   Garden clippers or scissors
>   Tape measure
>   Pencil and pencil sharpener
>   Bucket

Optional: *Spray Acrylic* (basket may be sprayed with a coat or two when it is completed)
Linseed Oil (*before* the basket is woven, the handles and rim may be treated with the oil to darken the color of the oak and bring out the grain)

Materials:
Hoops:
1   8" by 12" oak oval hoop, 1" wide
1   8" by 8" oak D–hoop, 1" wide

Ribs:
1 bundle #7 round reed

Dye (unless you choose not to use color):
1 package of each color — light blue, royal blue, lavender, and dark blue

Weavers:
1 bundle ³⁄₁₆" flat reed, natural color
1 bundle #2 round reed, for weavers

Dye the weavers as follows (or leave undyed for an all-natural look):

>   Light Blue: 6 strands #2 round reed
>   Lavender: 4 strands #2 round reed
>   Dark Blue: 6 strands #2 round reed
>   Royal Blue: Half the bundle of flat reed

   If you would like to weave the basket in natural, omit the dyes and the #2 round reed.

Step 2. Four-Fold Lashing

To secure the two hoops together, a four-fold lashing must be made. (See the instructions for four-fold lashing that begins on page 3.) It will hold the two hoops together and create a resting place for the basket's ribs. As you weave the lashing, which will form both the side and the bottom of the basket, you must force the reed down toward the bottom of the basket with your fingertips to create a flat bottom.

First, soak a long piece of ³⁄₁₆-inch flat reed until it is pliable (four to five minutes) in a bucket of warm water. Do not soak the reed too long or it will crack and fray. Then begin the lashing.

Complete nine full rows of lashing, ending at the bottom of the D-hoop where you began. The rows can be counted along the back of the hoops. Be sure that the lashing bends down at the bottom of the basket and that there are no gaps between the rows.

16½-inch round reed

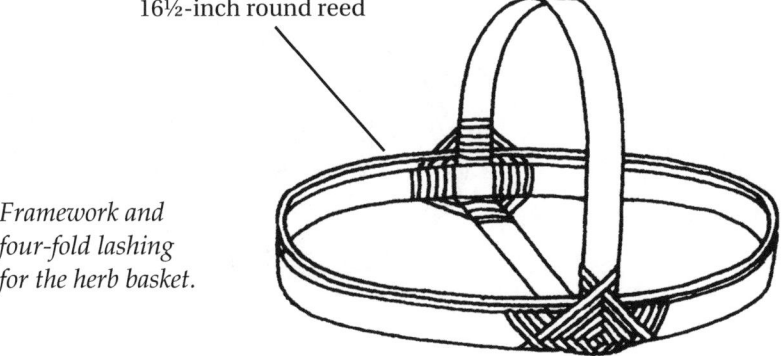

Framework and four-fold lashing for the herb basket.

Step 3. Structure

This basket requires ribs in the bottom of the basket only, as there are no real sides of the basket other than the rim. Widen the rim by adding a piece of #7 round reed along the top of each section of the rim. This also helps to tighten the weaving. To do this, cut two pieces of #7 round reed about 16½ inches long. Place one on each side of the basket, laying them on top of the rim with the ends resting behind the lashing.

The framework itself also uses #7 round reed. There will be only three ribs on each side of the basket bottom to begin with. Cut two sets of three each from #7 round reed in the following lengths:

First rib — 14½ inches long
Second rib — 11½ inches long
Third rib — 8 inches long

Taper each end of the ribs, or sharpen them with a pencil sharpener, so that they will fit snugly behind the lashing. The first rib is placed at the bottom near the rim. The second rib is placed in the center. The third rib is placed near the bottom section of the D-hoop.

Repeat the placement on the other side of the bottom of the basket with the second set of three ribs.

Rib placement for the bottom of the herb basket (view from the bottom).

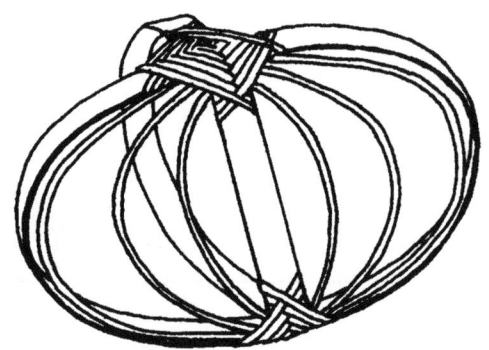

Step 4. Weaving

Begin the weaving with a soaked piece of ³⁄₁₆-inch flat natural reed. Tuck the end into the base of the lashing on the bottom of the basket with the right side facing out. Bend it over so that the wrong side is facing you and start the weaving toward the right. Weave under all three ribs, treating them as one unit. Then weave over the rim and under the extra rib at the top of the rim, wrap it around, and weave back down under the rim. Next weave over the three ribs and under the handle bottom. Continue to weave to the left side, going over the three ribs, under the rim, then over the rib at the top. Then wrap the reed around and go back down. Weave over the rim, under the three ribs, and over the handle bottom to where you began. You have now completed one full row of weaving. Repeat this one row on the other side of the basket. Be sure to bring the reed up close to the lashing so there are no gaps.

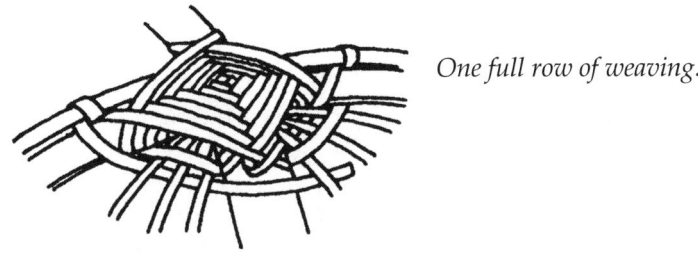

One full row of weaving.

Weave the next two rows by going under one rib, over the next, and under the third. Weave over the rim, under the top rib, wrap it around, and weave back down under the rim. Then weave over one rib, under the next, and over the last. Continue weaving under the handle bottom, over the rib toward the left, under the next rib, and over the last rib. Weave under the rim, over the extra rim piece, wrap it around, and weave back down over the rim. Then weave under the first rib, over the next rib, and under the last rib. Weave over the handle bottom to bring you back to where you began. Weave one more complete row in this manner. Then repeat these two rows on the other side of the basket. Each side should now have three complete rows of weaving in the flat natural reed.

If you run out of reed, it will be necessary to add in a new soaked piece of ³⁄₁₆-inch flat reed to complete the three rows described above. Lay the new weaver on top of the old one so that they overlap for a couple of inches. Tuck the end of the new piece under a rib and weave it along with the old piece. Then continue the weaving with the new piece (see box on page 17).

You will find that the right and wrong sides of the reed alternate with every row. One row will have the right side up and the next row will have the wrong side up. Be sure that the outer face of the new piece of reed matches the old one.

Step 5. Additional Ribs

It is now necessary to add some extra ribs to the framework of the basket. This is a fairly small basket, so this will be the only addition of ribs necessary. Three ribs need to be added to each side. Cut two sets of three ribs each from #7 round reed in the following lengths:

> First rib — 11 inches long
> Second rib — 9 inches long
> Third rib — 7 inches long

The 11-inch rib should be placed between the first and second original ribs. The 9-inch rib should be placed between the second and third ribs. The 7-inch rib should be placed between the third rib and the handle bottom. Cut the ends of the ribs at an angle so that they can slide into the weaving and rest evenly next to each rib.

Place the other three ribs on the other side of the basket bottom. There should now be a grand total of twelve ribs in the basket.

Placement of additional ribs.

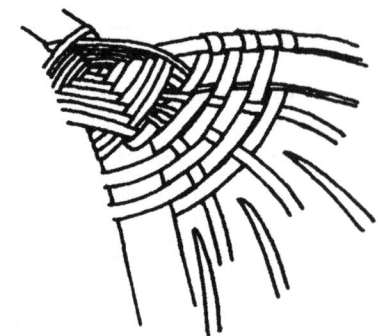

Step 6. Color

The blue color pattern is now introduced into the basket. Or, if you wish, you may continue to weave with the flat natural reed for the entire basket.

If you continue with the natural reed, simply continue to weave with the piece of ³⁄₁₆-inch flat natural reed, weaving over the new ribs and adding new weavers as necessary. Continue to follow the rest of the directions for the basket, ignoring the color pattern.

If you are adding the color pattern, cut the piece of flat reed so that it extends slightly beyond the bottom portion where you ended the third row (see illustration on page 16).

Start with a soaked piece of light blue #2 round reed. Place the end of the round reed under the rib to the left of the handle bottom, laying it right next to the flat natural reed. As you continue the weaving, be sure to include the new ribs. Weave under one rib to your right, over the next rib, and under the next rib in the usual over-and-under pattern. Complete three full rows ending at the handle bottom. Cut the reed with a few extra inches of overlap. Then repeat the three rows of light blue on the other side.

Continue weaving the rest of the pattern by following the chart below. Be sure to do the same number of rows on each side of the basket.

Color Pattern Chart

3 rows — natural flat reed
3 rows — light blue round reed
2 rows — lavender round reed
3 rows — dark blue round reed
1 row — natural flat reed

The rest of the basket is then woven in royal blue flat reed.

Step 7. Filling In

The space at the handle bottom gets woven in very quickly. You will need to do some filling in on both sides of the basket to allow the last few rows of weaving to be done straight across the basket, from one rim to the other.

Because of the irregularities of the hoops and each individual's weaving style, this part of the weaving may be difficult. A certain amount of judgment on your part will be required.

Proceed with the weaving toward the right side. Weave to the rim, but only weave back down as far as the fourth rib. Wrap the reed around that rib and weave back up toward the rim again. Weave around the rim, back down to the third rib, and then back up to the rim. Repeat this again and wrap the next row around the second rib. Weave around the rim and then back down through all the ribs to the other side of the handle bottom. Repeat this filling-in process on the left side of the basket (see illustration on page 20 for an example of filling in). Be sure to do an equal amount of filling in on the other side of the basket, so that the weaving is balanced.

When each side has been filled in, you should be able to complete the weaving with three or four rows on each side of the basket. The weaving from each side should meet in the center where each end of the reeds can be overlapped, just as when new weavers are added to one another. If you still find a gap on each side, you should add another row or two of weaving.

The handle on this basket is left natural, as the oak is too attractive to cover.

Step 8. Finishing

Trim any stray ends of pieces of reed that remain. The basket can be given a coat of acrylic spray to help protect it and preserve the color. The handle of this basket also looks much nicer if it is given a coat of linseed oil. This brings out the grain of the wood and darkens it slightly.

Sources and Suppliers

The Caning Shop
800-544-3373
www.caningshop.com

Connecticut Cane & Reed Co.
www.caneandreed.com

The Country Seat Inc.
610-756-6124
www.countryseat.com

H. H. Perkins Co.
800-462-6660
www.hhperkins.com

Royalwood Ltd.
800-526-1630
www.royalwoodltd.com

Suzanne Moore's N. C. Basket
Works, Inc.
800-338-4972
www.ncbasketworks.com

V. I. Reed & Cane, Inc.
800-852-0025
www.basketweaving.com

Basket Makers' Associations

Many basket makers' associations have been formed to help pro-
mote the knowledge of basket weaving. They often offer work-
shops, seminars, and conventions where learning, encouragement,
and friendships can flourish. Contact a local art center or craft shop
to find out about basket makers' associations in your area.

Other Storey Titles You Will Enjoy

The Knitting Answer Book, 2nd Edition
by Margaret Radcliffe
Knitters of all levels will find solutions to their knitting problems in this essential reference. The easy-to-use Q & A format covers everything from casting on and binding off to reading patterns, managing multiple colors, finishing, and more.

The Sandalmaking Workshop
by Rachel Corry
Learn to create your own custom sandals in just a few hours. Accessible instructions walk you through every step of the sandalmaking process, from choosing leather and purchasing tools to adding laces or buckles and adjusting the fit.

Shell Chic
by Marlene Hurley Marshall
Creative works and design ideas from today's shell artisans, in full-color photography.

Soap Crafting
by Anne-Marie Faiola
Full-color step-by-step instructions and explorations on the full range of special effects that can be achieved in a bar of soap.

Woodland Style
by Marlene Hurley Marshall
Inspiration and projects to use responsibly collected materials to create stylish home décor.

Join the conversation. Share your experience with this book, learn more about Storey Publishing's authors, and read original essays and book excerpts at storey.com.

ᴊur books wherever quality books are sold or by calling 800-441-5700.